The Stendhal Syndrome

Other works by Terrence McNally

Plays

*And Things That Go Bump in the Night • Cuba Si • Next
Morning, Noon, and Night • Sweet Eros and Witness
Tour in "Collision Course" • Where Has Tommy Flowers Gone?
Whiskey • Bad Habits • The Ritz • It's Only a Play
Frankie and Johnny in the Clair de Lune • Faith, Hope, and Charity
The Lisbon Traviata • Lips Together, Teeth Apart • A Perfect Ganesh
Love! Valour! Compassion! • By the Sea, by the Sea, by the Beautiful Sea
Master Class • Five Short Plays • Corpus Christi
Some Christmas Letters • House (written with Jon Robin Baitz)
Let It Bleed • Short Talks on the Universe: Ghost Light
The Wibbly, Wobbly, Wiggly Dance That Cleopatterer Did*

Musicals and Operas

*The Rink • Kiss of the Spider Woman • Ragtime • The Full Monty
The Visit • A Man of No Importance
Central Park (The Food of Love) (written with Robert Beaser)
Dead Man Walking (written with Jake Heggie)*

Screenplays and Teleplays

*Apple Pie • Botticelli • Last Gasps • Positively Tenth Street
The Five Forty-Eight • Mama Malone
The Education of Young Harry Bellair, Esq., or The Way of the World
Puccini • Native Tomatoes/Local Peaches
Sam Found Out or the Queen of Mababawe (written with Wendy Wasserstein)
Andre's Mother • Trying Times II: L/S/M/F/T
Frankie and Johnny in the Clair de Lune • Sand between the Sheets
The Last Mile • Common Ground (Mr. Roberts) • The Ritz
Love! Valour! Compassion!*

TERRENCE McNALLY

The Stendhal Syndrome

Full Frontal Nudity

Prelude & Liebestod

Grove Press
New York

Published simultaneously in Canada
Printed in the United States of America

FIRST EDITION

Library of Congress Cataloging-in-Publication Data

McNally, Terrence.
    The Stendhal syndrome / by Terrence McNally.— 1st ed.
       p. cm.
    Contents: Full frontal nudity — Prelude & Liebestod.
    ISBN 0-8021-4150-1
       1. Michelangelo Buonarroti, 1475–1564. David—Drama.   2. Americans—Italy—Drama.
    3. Florence (Italy)—Drama.   4. Wagner, Richard, 1813–1883—Appreciation—Drama.
    5. Conductors—Drama.   I. McNally, Terrence. Full frontal nudity.   II. McNally, Terrence.
    Prelude & Liebestod.   III. Title.

    PS3563.A323S88 2004
    812'.54—dc22   2004054362

Grove Press
841 Broadway
New York, NY 10003

04 05 06 07   10 9 8 7 6 5 4 3 2 1

For Richard Thomas

The Stendhal Syndrome had its world premiere at Primary Stages, New York City, on February 15, 2004. Casey Childs, executive producer, and Andrew Leynse, artistic director, in association with Ted Snowdon. The cast was as follows:

Full Frontal Nudity

BIMBI   Isabella Rossellini

LANA   Jennifer Mudge

HECTOR   Michael Countryman

LEO   Yul Vázquez

Prelude & Liebestod

CONDUCTOR   Richard Thomas

CONDUCTOR'S WIFE   Isabella Rossellini

YOUNG MAN   Yul Vázquez

CONCERTMASTER   Michael Countryman

SOPRANO   Jennifer Mudge

Directed by Leonard Foglia; Tyler Marchant, associate director; Michael McGarty, set design; David C. Woodland, costume design; Russell H. Champa, lighting design; David Van Tieghem, original music and sound design; Laurie Marvald, prop design; Renee Lutz, production stage manager; Tammy Scozzafva, assistant stage manager; Lester P. Grant, production manager; Stephanie Klapper, casting; and Andrea Lepcio, production assistant.

The Stendhal Syndrome

FULL
FRONTAL
NUDITY

Time: The present.

Place: Florence, Italy, the Accademia Gallery, where Michelangelo's
David *is on display.*

Lights up.

We are in the Accademia Gallery in Florence.

At first we hear the sounds of a crowded gallery. French, Italian, German, Japanese—all are being spoken.

The voices fade as the lights come up on four people, two men and two women.

They stand facing us. They are looking at Michelangelo's David, *which is projected on a screen behind them. There is an appropriate moment of awed silence.*

BIMBI, *the tour guide, is first to speak.*

BIMBI *Ecco,* the *David.* I don't think I have to say anything, do you? What would be the point? Words would only diminish this experience. I'll just let you take it in. Are you astonished? Are you even breathing still? Listen to your heart, not me. Imagine you're alone with him.

HECTOR (All your life you dream of this moment and then it's here and part of you thinks you could die from it and part of you thinks, So what? There should be two of us standing here.)

BIMBI Coming here every day, sometimes twice, six days a week, fifty-two weeks a year, and it takes my breath away every time!

LANA (I get what's going on here: male pornography. Objectifying the male of the species for a change. I love it. Show us everything you've got, honey. Hot stuff, yeah! Oh God, there go my nipples.)

BIMBI *Che bello, eh? Che perfezzione! Che meraviglia!*

LEO (I don't see what the big deal is. I've got a bigger dick. I mean, proportionately bigger. If I were his size, mine would be bigger. Well maybe not bigger but certainly *as* big. That's a load off my mind. I was expecting this guy to totally wipe me out in that department.)

BIMBI (*to* LEO)   A penny for your thoughts, signore.

LEO   He's got weird pubic hair. It's in big wavy clumps, like maybe somebody gave him a perm down there. Real pubic hair isn't like that.

BIMBI   Let's return to our silent contemplation, shall we? (The worst part of my job is asking people what they think because then I have to listen to what they think.)

LEO   (What did I say? You gonna tell me I'm the only person looking at his dick? What else am I supposed to look at?)

BIMBI   Let the divine genius of Michelangelo take you to another plane. One of silent contemplation, ecstasy even.

LANA   Excuse me, but what time—

BIMBI   Don't speak yet, signora. Take it in. Look, feel. Then ask questions.

LANA   (I was just going to ask when lunch was. What a bitch.)

LEO   (She caught your eye again. Maybe she wants me. That's why women take these trips. To get some culture and to score. Hell, that's the reason men take these trips. Go for it, man.)

BIMBI   Just look at the head alone. The detail. The line. Already I'm saying too much, signora.

We see a close-up of the head. As we continue we will see close-ups of specific features: the eyes, the nose, the lips, etc.

LANA   It's signorina.

BIMBI   Ah, signorina. I couldn't tell, Miss Turner.

LANA   And I'm afraid it's not Turner, either. It's Maxwell. *Signorina* Lana Maxwell. Not every Lana is a Turner and not every Turner is a Lana. Sometimes we're just a Maxwell.

BIMBI   Again, my apologies.

LANA   That's all right. I get Turner a lot from older people. And you are?

BIMBI   Bimbi.

LANA   Bimbi?

BIMBI   Just Bimbi.

LANA   Oh, like bimbo, only it's Bimbi. I don't know what my mother was thinking when she named me. Of course, most people my age don't even know who Lana Turner is or was. I'm sure she's dead by now.

BIMBI   She died at least ten years ago.

LANA   She must have been a hundred. What happened?

BIMBI   I don't know. Cancer, old age, cirrhosis of the liver— the way we all go if we're not lucky.

LEO (*seeing his opportunity*)   No, no, no, no, no. She was murdered by her lover. He was this small-time Italian Mafia thug. He cut her throat and got blood all over this big white rug she had in her bedroom. The Lifetime Channel did a whole big thing on it.

LANA   You've got it all wrong. She murdered her lover and her daughter, Cherry Something Crane, took the rap for her and served time in prison and then worked as a restaurant hostess when she got out, but now she's a lesbian and lives in Palm Springs with her girlfriend and they raise dogs. Dachshunds, I think, but definitely some kind of dogs.

LEO   At least I got the bedroom and the white rug and the gangster right.

HECTOR   (I shall go mad if this keeps up.)

LANA   Some people think the lover had been having an affair with the daughter, which is why Lana killed him.

BIMBI   This would have been before the daughter was a lesbian, of course.

LANA   Maybe it was the reason she turned lesbian. Or maybe it was in prison she turned.

LEO   That can happen. Same with guys. Keeps me on the straight and narrow. End up some black dude's prison bitch, no way!

HECTOR   (I am going mad with these people.)

BIMBI   He was having an affair with the daughter.

LANA   That's never been proven.

BIMBI   Of course he was. He was an Italian. If he'd been having an affair with the mother, there was no motivation. In Italy, if you sleep with the daughter, you're going to be murdered by the mother.

LANA   This was in Beverly Hills.

BIMBI   Even in Beverly Hills.

HECTOR   (No, I have gone mad!) Could we please concentrate on the sublime work of art in front of us and stop this inane conversation about Hollywood? We're in Florence, for Christ's sake. You're the tour guide. Can't you control these people? Thank you.

BIMBI   I tell people what they're looking at, signore, not what to say.

HECTOR   Then tell us something—anything to shut that woman up.

LEO   Hey! That's no way to talk to a lady.

BIMBI   The signore has a point. Perhaps we have strayed too far from the *David*.

HECTOR   Thank you. *Grazie.*

LEO   (I bet that guy's gay. That type usually is. What is it about me that attracts them?)

BIMBI   Now, do we all know who David was?

LEO   You means he's not just a statue called David?

LANA   I think she means in real life.

BIMBI   David was an Old Testament hero who defeated the giant, Goliath, and so saved his people from the Philistines.

LEO   I've heard of them. They've got a great basketball team. The Pittsburgh Philistines. Hi.

LANA   Hi.

LEO   That was a joke.

LANA   I know.

BIMBI   Michelangelo shows David as an athletic youth, completely naked.

LEO (*for Lana's benefit*) We're paying her good money to tell us he's butt naked?

LANA *Sshh!* Don't. I'll get the giggles.

BIMBI Notice with what quiet concentration he turns his head to his left, directing his self-confident gaze toward his approaching opponent.

LEO Yeah, she's right. See that? His head *is* turned.

BIMBI Only his furrowed brow reveals the fierce concentration with which he regards the approaching enemy.

LEO See the furrow? This is cool.

BIMBI For the Florentines, the unveiling of the statue in the heart of the Piazza della Signoria must have been a sensation.

LEO I'll bet it was. People must have shit themselves. (Don't give me that look, Liberace.) (*to Lana*) You have dinner plans?

LANA We're on a tour. You don't make dinner plans on a tour. You eat with the tour. Haven't you ever traveled before?

LEO Not with you.

BIMBI Moreover, this naked "giant" was a completely nontraditional rendering of a traditional Renaissance subject. Where was his armor? His sword? Where was his shield?

LEO Going into battle with your willy exposed! Now that's what I call feeling vulnerable!

LANA Stop, I said.

BIMBI In contrast to traditional portrayals of the historical David, Michelangelo's *capalavoro* is to be understood not as a symbol of victory and might but as an embodiment of youthful strength and self-confidence.

HECTOR And masculine beauty.

LEO (Go on, tell us you're not gay, darling.)

LANA What's a *capo*-something?

LEO Hunh? I wasn't listening.

BIMBI Michelangelo began the *David* in 1501. It took him four years to complete.

LANA Four years! I couldn't do something like that in four centuries!

LEO I don't think that's the point. People like us aren't supposed to do anything like that ever.

BIMBI The *David* was originally intended for placement high above the spectator. Hence the exaggerated size of the head. When the city fathers decided to place the *David* in the Piazza della Signoria, Michelangelo had to rework the back so the statue could be viewed from all sides. Two dimensions becoming three.

LANA Do you know what's she talking about?

LEO She lost me back at the Ponte Vecchio. (She definitely wants me.)

LANA (Why do I feel like he's coming on to me? I thought he was gay.)

BIMBI The block of marble had already been partly worked by others and as a result there were severe restrictions on what Michelangelo could do with it.

HECTOR I didn't know that—about the marble being previously worked.

BIMBI However, these limitations did not prevent Michelangelo from depicting David *contraposto*—a pose in which the body's weight rests on one leg, the shoulders being at an angle to the hips, a posture that lends a figure animation.

HECTOR I see, I see.

BIMBI Try it yourself.

Hector shifts his weight to one leg.

HECTOR This is very informative. Thank you.

BIMBI I think I sound like a textbook.

HECTOR Not at all. Your delivery is very spontaneous and charming.

BIMBI Actually, they make us memorize all that in five languages.

HECTOR If the other four are as good as your English . . .

BIMBI You don't want to catch me when I'm leading a group of Japanese tourists. The other day I told them to pay especial attention to the Virgin Mary's liver.

Bimbi and Hector share a laugh.

LEO (What is it with women and gay men? Why do they like them? I don't get it.)

BIMBI David originally stood outside the Palazzo Vecchio, the site of the city's government, but was moved indoors to its present location in 1873. Does anyone have an idea why it was moved?

LANA Don't look at me.

LEO I'll take a shot.

HECTOR (This should be good.)

LEO There were too many automobile accidents. You're driving along, minding your own business, when all of a sudden you see this big naked guy in the middle of the road. A sight like that, you could lose complete control of your vehicle. At least I would and I'm straight. Can you imagine some gay guy seeing that for the first time?

BIMBI What's your point?

LEO Traffic in this country is bad enough without some guy's wiener looming over your dashboard. Imagine if you were a lady driver—and I'm not making women drivers jokes!—and there you are in your little Fiat 300. Your husband hasn't given it to you in months, you're coming home from a soccer match, all those hot sweaty men, and you see that thing straight ahead of you. You're gonna look where you're driving? I don't think so. More blood and gore on the *autostrada!* Or a young girl. Dig this: She's a virgin, out for her very first drive. Why she hardly knows where the fucking brake is—pardon my language but I'm getting very emotional—when she gets a load of our friend here. She's never seen a naked man. Put yourself in her place. D.O.A. The poor kid never had a chance.

BIMBI I'm speechless, Mr.—

LEO Sampson. Leo Sampson. Sampson's the name and mighty is the frame.

HECTOR (This man could potentially murder us all.)

BIMBI Unfortunately, your Mr. Henry Ford didn't invent the automobile until considerably after the *David* had been moved indoors.

LEO All right, so he was frightening the *horses.* I mean, you know, this old-time sixteenth-century horse is minding his business, clopping along, clop-clop-clop, he—or *she!* We all know the P.C. drill—our Renaissance imaginary hermaphrodite horse comes around a corner and finds him/her/itself face-to-face with our naked friend and his uncircumcised dick here! What would you do if you were a horse?

BIMBI I don't know.

LEO You'd bolt, lady. You'd rear up on your hind legs and throw your rider to his death, a broken neck. This goes on for a century or two until the town fathers in all their Renaissance wisdom say, "We better haul this sucker indoors before more innocent Florentines are killed by the sight of this guy's johnson." That's black American slang for "penis."

BIMBI Thank you.

LEO What do you say, teach? Do I go to the head of the class?

BIMBI You have a vivid imagination, Mr. Sampson.

LEO Thank you.

HECTOR It wasn't a compliment. The *David* was moved indoors because of the ravages of the elements. Snow, ice, wind, rain.

LANA You mean, like acid rain?

HECTOR Yes.

LEO Blow it out your ass: acid rain! They didn't have acid rain in the nineteenth century any more than they had cars.

HECTOR They had the equivalent of acid rain.

LEO That's *my* point: Horses were the equivalent of cars.

HECTOR Maybe, just maybe, horses were the *precursor* of the automobile, but by no stretch of the imagination or semantics can they be called the *equivalent*.

LEO I'm not going to get into little word games with you.

HECTOR Good, you'd lose!

LEO I rest my case.

HECTOR What case? You have no case. You have proposed something as idiotic as it is wrong.

LEO I am definitely being insulted by this asshole.

HECTOR "Sampson is the name and mighty is the frame."

LEO These intellectuals! They'll do it to you every time: look down their noses at you. "Ineffectuals" is what I call 'em. All bark, no bite. They don't even bark. It's just talk.

HECTOR I had your number the moment we left the hotel.

LEO I'm frightened. What number would that be?

HECTOR When you took the front seat in the minivan without even asking.

LEO I always sit in the front.

HECTOR A gentleman would have asked, "Would anyone care for the front seat?" before just appropriating it for himself. You plopped yourself right in, as if we were invisible.

LEO I didn't plop anywhere. I saw the seat was empty, I took it.

HECTOR You plopped.

LEO I did not plop. What are you laughing at?

LANA Grown men behaving like children.

LEO He started it.

LANA He did not.

LEO He did, too.

LANA He did not.

LEO He did, too.

LANA He did not!

HECTOR *Aaaarrgh!!!*

BIMBI I think we're upsetting the gentleman. What's wrong, signore?

HECTOR What's wrong? What's wrong? Bell'Italia Tours has a lot to answer for. "See Italy and die," your ad said. No, it should read, "See Italy with those two and drop dead while you're actually there."

BIMBI Let me deal with them.

LEO Now we've both been insulted.

BIMBI Mr. Charlotte is a professor of English who's taken early retirement.

LEO That's no excuse.

BIMBI You don't understand. His wife died recently after a long illness. His son was killed in a car accident on their way to the funeral.

LANA Oh my God. That's terrible.

BIMBI Mr. Charlotte was driving. The driver of the other car was drunk.

LEO Why didn't you tell us? I feel about this big now.

BIMBI So I think we all have to bear in mind such suffering when we consider what a pain in the ass he is.

LEO I am so, so sorry about your loss, man.

HECTOR Thank you.

LEO I had no idea. I take back everything I said. One thing about me, I don't hold a grudge. Put it there. (*They shake hands.*) I'm going to say a prayer for the two of them at the next church we visit. Your wife and your son. And you, too. Hell, I'll say a prayer for all of us.

HECTOR Thank you.

LEO I'm not as bad as I seem.

HECTOR Most people aren't.

LANA You speak such wonderful English for an Italian.

BIMBI   I'm not an Italian. My father was Albanian, my mother was Greek. I was born in the Philippines but I grew up in Perth. My first husband, Svet, was Swedish. After we got married, we emigrated to Norway, where we were living in Ulberg (Ulberg is about seventy kilometers from Oslo; it's famous for its luggage factory), which is where and when I met my present husband, Gian Carlo Noni, a well-known and much respected journalist with *Il Messagero,* one of our daily newspapers. I left Svet and Norway for Gian Carlo and Italy, and we've lived *qui,* here in Firenze, ever since.

LANA   *Qui? "Qui"* means "here"?

BIMBI   *Brava!*

LANA   It was just a guess. But I love speaking Italian. It seems so easy. But I guess it does get harder if you want to get really good at it?

BIMBI   I'm afraid so. I'm still struggling with the past perfect subjunctive.

LANA   Everything gets harder if you really want to be good at it. Start with marriage.

BIMBI   I'm sorry.

LANA   Maybe I should have gone to that Ulberg instead of Italy.

BIMBI   There's no right place to look for love, signorina, but as your American songs says: many, many wrong ones. (*to Hector*) You seem lost in a dream, Mr. Charlotte.

HECTOR   I've waited a lifetime for this.

BIMBI   It looks like our friend is having an ecstatic experience.

HECTOR   I'm sorry.

BIMBI   Nonsense. It's what we've all come here for.

HECTOR   I thought I'd seen the *David* before—in pictures and reproductions—but I realize I hadn't really seen him at all.

BIMBI   Yes.

LEO   Maybe we both should have gone to that Ulberg.

LANA   I'd come home with a new suitcase and frostbite.

LEO   Me, too.

LANA   At least in Italy you're warm. And I just bought a new suitcase for this trip.

LEO   You're divorced?

LANA   Legally separated, whatever that means.

LEO   It means you're still married but not responsible for each other financially or for any legal documents you might sign. I speak from bitter experience. Yours was a bastard and mine was a bitch. They didn't deserve us.

LANA (*bursting into tears*)   Now look what you've made me do. I haven't done that since I got off the plane.

LEO   I'm sorry. When I like someone: I try to get a little smile out of them. It seems we're in the same boat.

LANA   For a nice man, you're not very sensitive, Mr. Salmon.

LEO   It's Sampson, like the Biblical hero. You know, Sampson and Delilah. Hear the *p*? Not Salmon, like the fish.

LANA   Oh, I wondered! "Salmon's the name and mighty is the frame." I mean, how mighty can a fish's frame be?

LEO   Maybe he wasn't a bastard, but he sure was a fool.

LANA   Lex always said it took two to tango.

LEO   Who's Lex?

LANA   My first husband. Don't ask.

LEO   I hope you told him it only takes one to screw up a marriage. So you think I'm nice?

LANA   Why? Are you trying to tell me you're not?

LEO   No, no. I'm not used to women thinking I'm nice. I'm used to them thinking I'm a jerk. Don't stop, I like it, I like it.

BIMBI   A lira for your thoughts, Signor Charlotte.

HECTOR   I could stand here forever and still not truly see it.

BIMBI   Sometimes I think we never really do.

HECTOR   I'm feeling completely humbled, just being in its presence.

BIMBI   As well you should, as well we all should.

HECTOR   It's perfect, it's sublime.

LEO   Can I clear something up? You said "my first husband"?

LANA   Well I certainly hope I'm not going to be single again the rest of my life. I like to think I still have my whole life ahead of me. Why do you think I'm taking this trip?

LEO   Me too, Lana; me too.

LANA   When in Rome, do as the Romans do.

LEO   We're in Florence.

LANA   I was hoping you weren't going to say that. (Men are so dumb. Women are dumb, too, but not like that.) I need an Orangina.

BIMBI   I'm afraid they don't sell refreshments in the gallery.

LANA   I don't know about anyone else but I think I've seen the *David*.

BIMBI   Are you sure? You may never pass this way again. Look again. Look hard, look deep, look long. That goes for you, too, Leo.

LEO   What am I looking for?

BIMBI   Beauty, a moment of truth, knowledge. Who knows? We might even see ourselves. Art is powerful.

Leo folds his arms and looks hard and long.

LEO   See me in him, huh? We're both Italian. We're men. We know how to stare down the enemy. But somehow I don't see him selling Toyotas in Pittsburgh.

BIMBI   Standing here in the Accademia, humbled by the presence of such a mighty achievement of human endeavor, who is not reminded of loss? How far we have fallen from what we might have been.

LEO   Show me someone who hasn't suffered loss and I'll show you someone who hasn't really lived. Someone who is . . . Help me, Lana, what's the word I want?

LANA   Incomplete?

LEO   That's the word. Incomplete. We all suffer. It's when we hide our wounds from one another that we get into trouble.

LANA That is so, so true.

HECTOR (We've gone from the *National Enquirer* straight to *The Oprah Winfrey Show*!)

BIMBI (I've got a bunch of Germans after lunch. Does anybody actually like the Germans?)

LEO (She's cooling on me, I can tell. I did something wrong. Shit! What was it?)

BIMBI Does anybody know the German for "I'm sorry, I couldn't get any vegetarian dinners"?

LANA "*Heil* Hitler" is the only German I speak.

BIMBI Watch what you say, Miss Maxwell.

LANA I'm not a Nazi. I just love to watch old war movies. That's where I got "Heil Hitler" from. But I'm not a Nazi. I'm not even a Republican. I don't know what I am. I have a question.

HECTOR (I tremble to hear it. All Florence trembles. All Europe.)

LEO (He's gonna start with her again!)

BIMBI I hope I can answer it.

LANA How old was David when he posed for Michelangelo?

HECTOR (It's the end of Western civilization as we know it!)

LEO (Jesus, even I know better than that.)

BIMBI What do you think?

LANA He looks young. He could be eighteen, twenty, but he could be in his thirties, too. He could be anything but old. I mean, he's not saggy anywhere, the way men get.

BIMBI   That's a very good answer.

HECTOR   Wait a minute! Wait a minute! What are you telling her? This is a statue of David from the Bible, the Old Testament. He was dead a couple of thousand years at least before Michelangelo was even born.

LANA   How could he pose for him if he were dead?

HECTOR   He didn't pose for him, you nincompoop.

BIMBI   The Old Testament David was a real person. Michelangelo's David is an idealization, a memory, a dream of him.

LANA   You mean he just made his David up? This guy in the sculpture never existed? Michelangelo just dreamed him? Now I'm really impressed. I thought—You don't want to know what I thought.

HECTOR   (We're all ears.)

LANA   I thought there was this really gorgeous guy running around Renaissance Italy and his name was David Something-or-other and Michelangelo put him in a big vat of plaster and made a mold of him and then broke the mold off before he suffocated and then Michelangelo poured molten marble into the mold and then blew it up to larger than life size and that's how we got this incredible statue. The real David, the guy in the mold, got married, had kids, got fat eating too much pizza and died. But he lives forever in the beauty and joy of youth in this statue.

BIMBI   Except for the part about the mold, you pretty much put your finger on it.

LANA   I wish I could.

BIMBI   What do you mean?

LANA   I have this urge to touch him. Run my fingers all over him.

BIMBI   We all do.

LEO   Speak for yourself, ladies. I don't want to touch some strange guy's butt. Hell, I don't even want to touch some guy-I-know's butt.

BIMBI   There used to be a lifeguard with legs like that at the beach in Rimini. We all wanted to run our fingers along his beautiful, beautiful legs.

LANA   An Italian lifeguard! That sounds funny. You don't think of Italians as having lifeguards.

BIMBI   Why not?

LANA   You seem so alive, so unafraid of death.

BIMBI   We're not, Miss Maxwell.

LANA   So did you do it? Run your fingers along his beautiful, beautiful legs?

BIMBI   No, I lusted in silence.

LANA   Look but don't touch. That's the story of most of our lives.

BIMBI   After a while they had to let Giorgio go. That was his name, Giorgio. Too many young girls were pretending to drown, and then, when one young signorina actually succeeded, it was "Ciao, Giorgio."

LANA   You never?

BIMBI   I never even spoke to him.

LANA What a sad story.

BIMBI I suppose it is, but that was another lifetime ago.
"Nel mezzo del cammin di nostra vita
Mi ritrovai per una selva oscura
Che la diritta via era smarrita."

HECTOR What was that?

BIMBI Dante. You have Shakespeare, we have Dante. I don't know why that came into my head.

HECTOR Will you translate it for us?

BIMBI It's not the same in English.

HECTOR Try.

BIMBI "In the middle of our life, I found I was on the wrong way in a dark wood." No, the wrong path. In other words, I'd lost my way. That's terrible, I'm sorry. All the poetry is gone. I'm sorry, Dante, *Mi scusi.*

HECTOR That's all right, I think we got the jist of it.

BIMBI I was alone here in the gallery one night. Alone with David. The guards, they all know me, they knew I wasn't going to take an ax to him like that maniac did to the *Pietà* in St. Peter's in Rome.
 I stood looking up at him, my mouth was probably agape, being alone with such monstrous beauty. I wanted to touch him so badly. If he weren't placed so high above me I don't know where I would have put my hand. On his thighs probably. I stood like this, my arm raised toward him—helplessly, of course, many meters from his flesh—all right, his *marble,* but is there one of us who doesn't believe it's his flesh as well? I looked over my shoulder to make

sure I was alone. I was! No one! If I could find a way to climb up onto his pedestal . . . but I couldn't move. My body was paralyzed. Suddenly I didn't want to touch him. I was glad I couldn't. It would have been a sacrilege, a profanation.

LEO   I can understand that.

LANA   I don't. That's a story you could have dined out on the rest of your life.

LEO   It's a work of art. She didn't want to defile it.

LANA   If it's really a work of art, you can't defile it. It's greater than the sum of its parts.

HECTOR   (That's the first intelligent thing she's said all day. There's hope for her.) I have no desire to touch him. It would limit my experience of him to the feel of cool, inanimate marble against my hand. From here, he's alive. I can see the veins in his forearm pulsing, surging with the hot blood of youth, eager to do battle. If I touch him, he's just a piece of stone.

LEO   I see your point, too. That's one of my troubles: I see everyone's point and I end up not having one of my own.

LANA   I want to hear the end of your story. So, you're standing there, your arm frozen, ready to touch him.

BIMBI   I fainted.

LANA   You fainted?

BIMBI   When I fell, I hit my head on the base there. There was a cut on my scalp, some blood, a few stitches. I still have a little scar.

LEO   What made you faint?

BIMBI The Stendhal Syndrome.

LANA The what?

BIMBI It's called the Stendhal Syndrome. Are you familiar with it?

LEO It sounds like a movie. Bruce Willis in the Stendhal Syndrome.

BIMBI When the great French writer Marie-Henri Beyle— better known as Stendhal, of course—

HECTOR *The Red and the Black.*

BIMBI He visited the churches and museums of Florence, the very ones we will visit today, and he observed that some people, usually women, but not always, became over-stimulated by certain works of art—a Botticelli Venus, for example, or a Raffaello youth. These people became light-headed, giddy; some even fainted. This emotional/physical response to art we now call the Stendhal syndrome—when art speaks to something deeper in us than perhaps we understand. It can be the same with music. In the nineteenth century, the works of Richard Wagner often caused people to experience what felt like orgasms while listening to his compositions. *Tristan und Isolde,* for example, faces flushed, corsets were loosened, smelling salts were necessary. There was no hiding the intensity of their feelings. Just as nothing had prepared them for their first encounter with Wagner's chromatic harmonies, nothing ever really prepares us for the perfection of this. (*The four of them look at the David again. Extreme close-up of his right eye.* EXTREME. *So extreme it is abstract.*)

HECTOR If we really let a work of art in, if we embrace it totally, it should overwhelm us.

LANA Then we wouldn't be able to go about our daily business.

HECTOR Precisely.

LEO Wow! This is heavy stuff. This is what I came for. Right on.

BIMBI (They're looking, but will they ever know what they really see?)

LANA I don't want to be overwhelmed by art. I want to be overwhelmed by life.

HECTOR No, you don't. I *was* overwhelmed by life.

LANA I don't mean overwhelmed by tragedy like you were. I meant overwhelmed by happiness.

HECTOR So did I. Art's all that remains to me.

LANA Were you very happy?

HECTOR Very.

LANA That's so sad.

BIMBI (You're the sad one, Miss Maxwell.)

LANA What was her name?

HECTOR Violetta.

BIMBI Like the opera?

HECTOR Yes. Both her parents were fanatics.

BIMBI Italians?

HECTOR Germans.

BIMBI They're the worst. It's a wonder they didn't name her for someone in the *Ring Cycle*. Grimhild or Gutrune or something.

LANA There's an opera called Violetta?

HECTOR *La Traviata.*

LANA *La Traviata*! I've heard of that.

HECTOR The heroine is Violetta.

LANA What a beautiful name.

HECTOR She didn't think so. I called her Vi.

LANA Violetta is much prettier. Vi could be a thing. Viaduct. Viacom. "Honey, have you seen my Viagra?" Violetta could only be a woman. A beautiful woman. I bet she was, too.

HECTOR I thought so.

LANA That's the important thing. Who cares what other people think?

HECTOR I certainly don't.

LANA That's very wise of you.

She moves away from him.

HECTOR (That sounded harsh. She took it the wrong way. Say something to her. I can't. Yes, you can.)

LANA (See what you get for even talking to people, Lana? When do we eat? Don't they feed you on this tour?)

BIMBI Where are you with David, Mr. Sampson?

LEO   There's a guy at my gym who has abs like that. Everybody hates him.

HECTOR   I don't know about you but I'm getting hungry, Miss Maxwell.

LANA   I'm sorry, were you speaking to me?

HECTOR   I'm sorry, you were lost in David.

LANA   He's a good place to be lost. Easy on the eyes and you don't have to worry what he thinks of you.

BIMBI   What else, Mr. Sampson?

LEO   I'm thinking if that was me standing up there, you'd all turn your backs. I mean, who wants to look at this? I mean, we all look like this, which is why we don't want to look at it.

BIMBI   Is that really what you're thinking?

LEO   I'm thinking I never looked like that. How different my life would have been if I had. How I'm going to die and that frightens me and I know it shouldn't but it does and I can't imagine ever not being afraid of death. (Why are you telling them this?) I'm thinking it's hard not to hate such perfection. I'm thinking if I had a hammer, yeah, I might like to take a piece out of him—the tip of his nose, maybe— so there's some flaw, something to make him like the rest of us.

BIMBI   I'm sorry I asked you.

LEO   I'm being honest.

BIMBI   You're being brutal.

LEO   It's a fantasy.

BIMBI It's an ugly one.

LEO I'm not going to do it. (She hates me, too, now. They all hate me. You try to tell someone who you really are and they despise you. You show them a bullshit façade so they don't and you despise yourself).

BIMBI (You can lead these people to art but you can't make them understand. Pearls before swine. Come off your high horse, Bimbi. What makes you superior to these people? That you speak four languages? That you know the difference between a Fra Angelico and a Botticelli? That your husband loves you and you love him? So what? How does that make you better? Luckier, that's all, luckier. Different, yes; better, no. But I feel superior to them. I can't help myself. It's my delusion.) So, are we done with the *David*? As if we ever could be! But we still have the Duomo, Ghiberti's bronze doors, the Uffizi, and Cellini's *Perseus*.

LANA I'm not afraid to touch him.

BIMBI What's stopping you? Don't let me and that lifeguard on the beach at Rimini be an example. You'll end up a tour guide in Florence waiting to win the lottery.

LANA I'm sure it's not allowed.

BIMBI It's not. That's what makes it so delicious. Forbidden fruit is always the sweetest.

LANA Tell me about it!

BIMBI I can close my eyes and still see Giorgio's silken thighs. That's what the hair on them seemed like: silk. Make your fantasy real. Go on, the guard's not looking. He's eating his lunch.

LANA   I'm sure a buzzer or something would go off.

LEO   Like in *The Thomas Crown Affair*. I love that movie.

BIMBI   There's no buzzer. Besides, he's a friend of mine.

LANA   Really? You'd let me touch him?

BIMBI   I'm not going to stop you.

LANA   That's not quite the same thing.

HECTOR   I hope this is a joke. You're not going to let her put her hand on a work of art? Actually touch it?

LANA   It's a piece of cement for Christ's sake. You'd think it was made of spun glass.

HECTOR   Cement! It's Carrara marble. You don't even know what you'd be touching.

LANA   You were right about these intellectuals.

LEO   *Hmm?* (Was she talking to me? Shit, I missed it!)

HECTOR   It doesn't take an intellectual to know the difference between cement and carefully sculpted Carrara marble.

LANA   Is that like the difference between a rock and a hard place, professor?

HECTOR   I'm not going to stand here and let you defile a work of art.

LEO   Who's defiling? She's touching. How do you think Michelangelo sculpted it? With surgical gloves on? No! With his own two bare hands. Besides, what's it to you if she touches it?

HECTOR   She has oil on her hands.

LANA   I do not. What kind of person do you think I am? Oil on my hands!

HECTOR   Everyone has oil on their hands. It's natural. That's why we can't go around touching works of art every time we get the urge. Would you go up to a strange man and put your hand on his rear end?

LANA   The way strange men put their hand on mine? Of course not!

HECTOR   Well, show him the same respect.

LANA   He's a statue. I'm a real living person.

BIMBI   Last chance. He's finishing his sandwich.

LANA   If I do it, will someone take my picture touching it?

HECTOR   Flash cameras in the Accademia!

LANA   What's the point of doing something if there's no proof you did?

LEO   I'll take it. We'll spend the night in jail together.

HECTOR   (Are you going to let this happen?) I insist you don't do this.

LEO   You can insist all you want. Insisting ain't stopping.

BIMBI   Aren't you the tiniest bit tempted, professor?

HECTOR   Not in the least.

Extreme close-up of the face of the David *from an entirely different angle than before.*

BIMBI   I don't believe you. Everyone wants to touch such beauty. Only we don't feel worthy to.

HECTOR   Speak for yourself.

BIMBI   I was. I always do. Who do you speak for?

LANA   OK, here goes nothing. (*She puts her hand out. All she can reach is the* David's *pedestal.*) Oh.

BIMBI   Take the picture.

Leo fumbles with the camera.

HECTOR   Take the goddamn picture!

LEO   What did it feel like?

LANA   You were right not to touch it.

BIMBI   You understand now.

LANA   I felt so insignificant. Suddenly he seemed like a god.

BIMBI   Michelangelo saw the god in all of us. That was his genius.

HECTOR   All your life you stand for things, believe in them, rules, stop signs, one and one are two, and then someone does something as wrong, as outrageous, as putting her dirty hands on a work of pristine, sublime beauty—an artifact of the very culture of mankind—and nothing happens. The world doesn't come to an end, the statue doesn't collapse, no angry arm of retribution rises up to smite the miscreant down. It makes you wonder how frail all our rules and contracts are. Everything is hanging by a thread when you get right down to it. Everything.

BIMBI   I think all great artists understand that, too, and their work is their protest that it should be like this.

LANA   I'd like to go back to the hotel.

BIMBI We still have so much to see.

LANA Fine, I'll walk. Is there a ladies' room? My hands are kind of dirty.

BIMBI Just by the entrance.

LANA The next person who wants to touch the *David,* Bimbi: Don't let them.

She goes.

LEO (Go after her. Now's your chance.) I'll go with her. Don't worry, I'll catch up at the next stop.

BIMBI Are you sure you've seen enough of the *David,* Mr. Sampson?

LEO Not when you say it like that. Who could?

He goes.

BIMBI Would you like to be alone with him?

HECTOR Thank you. They were kind of noisy.

BIMBI I'm afraid I was, too, Mr. Charlotte.

HECTOR It's Hector, please.

BIMBI *David* does that to us. Why can't we just look at him and be thankful? I'll wait for you in the minibus. Our driver can get quite aggressive on the horn.

Bimbi goes.

HECTOR (What a stupid expression: minivan. They mini everything nowadays. Minivan, minibar, mini-me.) God, that expression on his face! From every angle it's different. Sometimes so fierce, at others so noble. All depends on

35

where you stand. I can't believe she did that. Touched the pedestal, even. God, how Michelangelo must have loved him to make him so beautiful. I could never imagine Vi being so beautiful. As much as I loved her, I always saw her breasts as they were, too large—even from the beginning—and I had begun to look the other way when she came out of the shower and I didn't want to see anymore how her body had thickened and sagged—not that it was ever perfect, like yours. I love you, Vi. I miss you. I don't know what I'm doing here without you. Our bed is so empty. So is my life. I miss Andrew, too, but not like you, not like you. What has he got in his hand? What is he holding? A rock, probably. Sure, a rock. He's David and he's going to put the rock in his sling and clobber . . . what's his name? Goliath! That's it, Goliath. Steve Reeves as Goliath. Whatever happened to him? Whatever happens to all of us? We die, unnoticed, unappreciated—yes, I have good qualities, Vi knew that, maybe she was the only one. I just don't care to share them with most people. Was that the dread minivan tooting?)

Leo returns.

LEO   She's a big girl. She'll get back to the hotel. I had to take one last look. It's so beautiful. (OK, asshole, don't acknowledge me.)

HECTOR   Yes, yes. *E bello. E molto bello.*

LEO   You can say that again.

HECTOR   We're very lucky to have had this experience. Something to tell your grandchildren.

LEO   I think I better have some children first. (He can be nice! Go figure.) I had a teacher in high school I looked up to, Mr. Moroney. He would be so happy to know I was standing here. Happy and surprised.

HECTOR Do you know whatever happened to Steve Reeves?

LEO Who?

HECTOR Sorry. Someone before your time.

Lana comes back in.

LANA You, too? One last look, hunh? I wasn't half a block from here when I said to myself, Where are you going, Lana? You have the rest of your life ahead of you, but you may never pass this way again.

The three of them are looking at the David. *They are becoming more and more statuelike themselves as they become more rapt in their concentration on the* David. *At the same time, the pictures of the* David *are getting smaller and smaller: His image is receding.*

LANA I love the veins in his hands. I had a boyfriend with veins in his hands like that. Right after we broke up, this was in high school, he turned into a junkie. Life is weird.

HECTOR (I love you, Vi. You're here with me. I feel your hand, I see your face.)

LEO (Don't be a jerk all your life, Leo. Take something away from this. Yeah, but what? How are you supposed to explain this? Maybe you don't have to.)

Bimbi returns.

BIMBI *Il minibus sta per partire.* That's Italian for the "minivan is leaving."

No one moves. Maybe we hear the minivan horn.

37

BIMBI (*cont.*)   Take your time, take your time.

Lights are starting to fade.

BIMBI (*cont.*)   It's your tour. We have all day. May I join you?

The four of them are still looking at the David *as the image of him continues to get smaller and smaller. Soon the image of the* David *has completely disappeared. The four of them are motionless like statues as the lights fade to black while the minivan continues to honk.*

THE END

PRELUDE
&
LIEBESTOD

Time: The present.

Place: The stage of a concert hall.

The lights come up on a conductor's podium, a small, square raised platform about fifteen inches high with a waist-high railing running the length of its upstage side.

Sounds of a symphony orchestra tuning up at random.

The stage is empty.

Spot up on a beautiful woman in a box seat somewhat upstage of the podium. She is the CONDUCTOR'S WIFE. *She is perfectly dressed and coiffed. She looks at her program. She looks at her wristwatch. She looks at the orchestra level below her. She looks up at the higher tiers and balcony above her.*

Spot up on a YOUNG MAN *in an orchestra-level seat, stage left, also somewhat upstage of the conductor's podium. He is looking at the Conductor's Wife through a pair of opera glasses. She is not aware of this.*

Spot up on an empty chair just to the downstage right of the podium. It belongs to the CONCERTMASTER. *He enters to a smattering of applause. He bows more than is necessary. He raps his bow on his violin stand and gives the note.*

An unseen symphony orchestra tunes up.

The Conductor's Wife opens her purse and takes out a small box of mints.

The Young Man continues to stare at her through his opera glasses.

The house lights dim in the concert hall where the Conductor's Wife and Young Man are sitting.

At the same time, the lights come up on the concert stage, i.e. the stage itself.

A spotlight hits the large doors leading to the backstage area through which one enters the stage itself. After a longer time than necessary (we should begin to wonder if something has gone wrong, in fact,) the doors are opened by unseen hands and the SOPRANO *enters to strong applause. She is in full concert diva regalia. A dress that doesn't stop, a stole, a jeweled collar of diamonds.*

As the Soprano moves toward her seat near the podium, she smiles at the unseen orchestra. The Concertmaster taps his bow on his stand in approval.

The Soprano turns her back to the orchestra (and us, in doing so,) and bows deeply to heavy applause.

Now the Soprano makes a great deal of arranging the panels of her gown and stole before she takes her seat. Her back will be to us but we will see her in profile as she turns from time to time to take a sip of water from a glass on a low table next to her chair or turns to the other side to smile at the Concertmaster.

Silence.

The spotlight has gone again to the double doors leading to the backstage area. It waits there. Again the doors are opened by unseen hands. No one appears.

Silence.

Someone coughs. Someone else shushes them.

The Concertmaster turns and looks to see what the hell is going on. He's seen it all before. He turns back.

CONCERTMASTER   Asshole.

The doors start to swing shut, then are suddenly pulled wide open as the CONDUCTOR *hurries through.*

Tumultuous applause. The Second Coming.

The Conductor moves swiftly to the podium and bows deeply. The Young Man has risen in his seat and is clapping wildly.

YOUNG MAN   Bravo! Bravo!

Conductor's Wife is applauding from her seat. Conductor leaps off podium and goes to Concertmaster and shakes his hand vigorously, then bear-hugs and kisses him. Ovation continues as Conductor crosses to Soprano and kisses her hand, then bear-hugs and kisses her. Young Man continues to stand and applaud.

YOUNG MAN   Bravo! Bravo, maestro!

Conductor's Wife has stopped applauding. Conductor has returned to podium for final bows to audience (which means his back is to us) as applause begins to diminish.

Young Man still stands and applauds. His voice is especially prominent as the general ovation continues to subside.

YOUNG MAN   Bravo! Bravo *il divino!*

Conductor looks to Young Man. Eye contact is made. Conductor's Wife looks at Young Man. Conductor looks up at his wife and smiles, then turns his back to the concert hall audience and faces his orchestra (us). Conductor is delighted with his reception. He gives orchestra members a self-deprecating grin and raises his eyebrows.

Silence.

He gets serious. He passes his hands over his face. He takes a deep breath. He raises his arms to begin. Young Man shatters the silence.

YOUNG MAN   We love you!

Conductor ignores this. Angry shushes from the audience. Conductor reaches to music stand in front of him and closes the open score. Gasps and whispers from the audience. He picks up baton again. He raises both arms. He waits. He tosses the baton onto his music stand and raises both arms again but this time he gives the downbeat almost at once.

Wagner's Prelude & Liebestod *from* Tristan und Isolde *is off and running.*

CONDUCTOR I love these pauses. That's right, you suckers, come on, play for me. Play through me, music. Surge. Course through me. Fill me up. Let me be you. Here it comes, this is it, the first crescendo . . . ! God, that was good. Now we're off and running. I'm up here already, that magic Olympian place. That was quick tonight. I like it up here. Who wouldn't? The view is glorious. So is the power. Fill, lungs. Heave, bosom. Burst, my heart.

From this point, the sound of the orchestra is considerably diminished and the Conductor will seem to be speaking from within his own private place. The music will be more a "surround" than a presence.

CONDUCTOR There were no empty seats. S.R.O. again, same as last week in Boston. There's no one more popular than me, is there? No one even close. We're number one and we don't try harder. What's that from? It's from something. Everything is from something. But not this. This music is not from anything. It's from God. This is the real thing. This is genius, this is still new, this is still shocking. God, I love Wagner! So shut up and conduct Wagner.

That one up there. I've seen him somewhere. Yeah, in your dreams, sweetheart. We don't do that anymore. You wanna bet? Oh shut up!

Hey, third cello, look at me! Yes, you! Where did they find you? Yes, you're too loud. You think I'd be looking at you like this if you weren't? (*He gives him the finger.*) Go tell your union I flipped you the bird in the middle of a

concert. I'll tell your union you played love music with a
chainsaw.

Jesus, where am I? Sometimes I think I do this on
automatic pilot. There we are, right on target! Saved again.
Somebody up there likes me. Yeah, Wagner. The Big Kraut
im Himmel himself. I've been good to Wagner and he's
been good to me.

I feel his eyes burning right into my back. He's mentally
undressing me. They all are. All 2,187 of them plus the 131
in standing room. Maybe I could steal a look at him. Are
you crazy? She's right up there in a box. She's always right
up there in a box. I'd like to see her in a box. It's her box
I'm sick of. You don't mean that. I don't mean that. You
love your wife. I love my wife. I love you. (*He looks over
his shoulder to his wife, who is reading something in her
program.*) She's reading! The fucking bitch is fucking reading
and you're conducting your fucking ass off. Jesus, I don't
know why I bother. Yes, you do. You wanted to be
married. No, you wanted to have children and you have to
be married to have children. No, you have to be married to
have children if you want to be the principal conductor of a
big symphony orchestra with a big stuffy endowment and
an even stuffier board of directors. You have to be beyond
reproach and so does Caesar's wife. You're only pissed off
right now because you've got the hots for some groupie and
your goddamn wife is right up there watching every move
you make. Who knew she had eagle eyes, bionic ears? She
can see and hear through lead walls if I'm talking to another
man. It's one thing to be straight, which I am, occasionally;
it's quite another to be in a straight jacket, which I am all
the time lately. Boston! That's where I saw him looking at
me like that! Last weekend in Boston, the all-Ravel

program. "The finest concert in this reviewer's half-century of concert-going." So sayeth the *Boston Globe*. He's following me. He's a stalker. You're not my first one, sweetheart, and you won't be my last.

(*suddenly aware of the Concertmaster*) What are you looking at, dogface? You didn't see me give you that cue? That's because you had your head up your ass. Don't give me that "It's your fault" look. I swear to God, sometimes I think he's calling me an asshole under his breath throughout an entire concert.

CONCERTMASTER   Asshole.

CONDUCTOR   There! Right now! I'm positive he's doing it.

CONCERTMASTER   The next Toscanini you're not. Hell, you ain't even the next Lenny Bernstein. You're the next asshole, period.

CONDUCTOR   I'd like to see you stand up here and lead an orchestra. Get eighty-seven musicians to play in tune and together. You think it's easy? Think again. Second strings, what the hell was that? I'm sure they all think—given the opportunity—they could conduct better than me. Sorry to disillusion you, minions. There's a reason I'm up here and you're down there. Genius. Sensibility. Je ne sais quoi. You either got it or you ain't, and Ladies and Gentlemen of the orchestra, I got it. Whoever said it's lonely at the top was right. No, it's lonely, period.

YOUNG MAN   Look at me. You know I'm here. You know where I'm sitting. I had the same seat in Boston. Take a look. You know you want to. Go on, I dare you. There's a climax coming. A quick glance over your left shoulder. Like you're in some sort of Wagnerian ecstasy and you have to pull away from the orchestra. You did it during the Ravel G Major. Our eyes met, for an instant, it was wonderful.

CONDUCTOR'S WIFE (*still looking at the program*)   Now that is what I call a stunning outfit. It would be perfect for the San Francisco opening night. He's always telling me I dress like a dowager. All right, darling, we'll go for the expensive hooker look. Who designed it? Oh, him! I should have guessed.

CONCERTMASTER   Asshole!

SOPRANO   Fuck you, too, mister.

CONCERTMASTER   I wasn't talking to you.

SOPRANO   What did I do to him? These instrumentalists, they all look down their noses at singers. Like they're the real musicians and we're the performing seals. I don't know where they get their attitude. There must be a course in it at Juilliard: "Basic Attitude for the First Violin." Look at him! What? I'm supposed to kill myself because I'm not Kirsten Fucking Flagstad or Birgit Fucking Nilsson or Jessye Fucking Norman! Well where are they right now? I'm the one up here getting ready to sing the fucking *Liebestod*! So get used to it, asshole.

CONCERTMASTER   I wasn't talking to you.

YOUNG MAN   It's coming. Now's your chance. Turn around. You know you want to.

CONDUCTOR   I feel his eyes on me. He's talking to you. Go ahead. This climax, it's the perfect place. She won't have a clue. Shit! I can't, the French horns are looking at me with that French horn "What do we do now?" look the French horns always give you in this passage. Too late, you blew it. I hate French horns.

YOUNG MAN That's all right, we've got the whole concert. This music is about sweet anticipation anyway. Now listen up while I whisper in your ear: You know what I'd do if I had you alone with me? I have it all planned. I'd undress you with my teeth. That's right, you heard me, I'd bite you out of that conductor's outfit. I'd start with your bow tie. I'd take one end of it in my teeth and pulllllllll it very slowly while it unraveled. And then I'd start with your shirt buttons. This button. (*He touches his collar button.*) Bite. (*He spits it out.*) Then the next button.

CONDUCTOR'S WIFE What's the point of having a cell phone if you have to turn it off most of the time? I told Ralph I'd call him at intermission. I want to talk to him now. Make plans for while the maestro's off in London. There's always that line at intermission. You either have to run for the ladies' room or make a telephone call. You can't do both. The maestro calls it my Hobson's choice. He can be very funny. I told Ralph what he called it and he said, "What's a Hobson's choice?" I felt like saying "Just shut up and fuck me, Ralph," but instead I explained very patiently what Hobson's choice was and by then Ralph had lost all interest in fucking me and was asking me if this were a Hobson's choice or that were a Hobson's choice. I told him, "Fucking me is a Hobson's choice," but he didn't get it. Ralph is my last lover from the current administration.

CONDUCTOR Turn, turn, turn. To everything there is a season. The Beatles? The Turtles? He'd know. Ten minutes with someone like that. Less even! It doesn't take long with someone like that. None of this Wagnerian attenuation. Just a nice fast Shostakovian bang-bang climax in the first eight bars. I want you so bad, house left.

CONCERTMASTER   He's lost. Bloody, bleeding, blooming asshole, you don't even know where you are in the music!

CONDUCTOR   Christ, what's next? (*To Concertmaster*) Thank you, thank you!

CONCERTMASTER   That's my, what, fourth save this season? You're welcome.

CONDUCTOR   Still, if I had a face like yours I'd kill myself.

SOPRANO   It's getting my turn. My throat's dry. I don't remember the words. I'm sweating like a Trojan. I'm sure there's lipstick on my teeth. Someone in the cellos just farted and I'm supposed to be in ecstasy. There's got to be a better way to earn a living.

The Prelude *is drawing to its quiet close.*

CONDUCTOR   How did we get to the end so fast? Christ, and people say Wagner is long! Come on, cow, it's your turn now. Give 'em what they came for.

Soprano stands and makes ready to sing: much arranging of dress, subtle throat clearings, etc.

CONDUCTOR   She's not a cow. Why did I call her that? She's quite pretty.

CONDUCTOR'S WIFE   I hear she's got a wonderful voice. He came home from rehearsals very excited. I wish someone would help her dress. Why do these women insist on wearing such unsuitable clothing?

SOPRANO God, what if I open my mouth and nothing comes out? They're all staring at me. What is it? My dress? I wish I were dead.

CONDUCTOR I love these last chords of the *Prelude*. Make 'em wait for the lights to come up. Make 'em wait for something to happen. Duh! Make 'em wait for the fat lady to sing. Duh! And silence. I love the silences! God, what a sense of theater.

This was spoken to the final chords of the Prelude. *Now the Conductor launches the* Liebestod *and cues the Soprano with a smile and a wink of encouragement.*

Soprano begins to sing. At first, the music and her voice will be at concert hall volume but then subside to the level of the Prelude. *Although her back is to us throughout the aria, it should be clear that the Soprano is deeply involved with singing and communicating with her audience out front. From time to time, she will turn her head to make eye contact with the Conductor. We will be hearing an excellent performance of the* Liebestod *from both of them.*

Surtitles will appear throughout.

SURTITLE *Mild und leise, wie er lächelt.*

CONDUCTOR'S WIFE Now that's a gorgeous voice.

SURTITLE *Wie das Auge hold er öffnet,*

CONCERTMASTER You're flat. Get up there, get up there!

YOUNG MAN Sharp as ever, wouldn't you know?

SURTITLE *Seht ihr's, Freunde? Säht ihr's nicht?*
  Immer lichter, wie er leuchtet,

Stern-umstrahlet hoch sich hebt?
Seht ihr's nicht?

CONDUCTOR   I told you in rehearsal: You're singing through the wrong hole, honey. This is twat music. Listen to it. Listen to the words. You're not singing, you're coming! God, if I had your instrument, they'd be dying out there.

SOPRANO   Don't listen to him. He can wave his arms all he wants but you're going to sing this piece the way you were taught, not like some banshee. Place the tone properly. Support it with your full diaphragm. Always legato. Just like they taught you at Juilliard. Thatta girl.

CONDUCTOR'S WIFE   To be able to sing like that! What a gift! What joy!

YOUNG MAN   They like her. They actually like her.

CONCERTMASTER   There you go, miss. That's more like it. Keep it up. I'm right here with you.

CONDUCTOR   Do you know what this music is about? It's about love. It's about dying. Don't give me that look of terror, sweetheart. It's too late for that. This isn't the classroom. This is the real thing. We're making love up here. We're gonna have a trans-fan-fucking-figuration. So sing it like you meant it!

SURTITLE   *Wie das Herz ihm muttig schwillt,*
Voll und hehr im Busen ihm quillt?
Wie den Lippen, wonnig mild,
Süsser Atem sanft entweht—
Freunde! Seht!
Fuhlt und seht ihr's nicht?

CONDUCTOR   Wagner knew a lot about fucking. I bet that guy up there does, too. If not, I'd be happy to teach him. I taught my wife. I'd like to fuck the entire world. No, I'd like to fuck every attractive man, woman, and child in the world. Child over fourteen. Better make that fifteen. No, sixteen. Fuck it.

CONCERTMASTER   What is he doing now?

CONDUCTOR   You're behind, everybody. Catch up, catch up!

SOPRANO   This is not the tempo we rehearsed.

CONDUCTOR   It's called inspiration, sweetheart.

YOUNG MAN   He's losing you, lady!

CONDUCTOR'S WIFE   There's a man over there who has Ralph's mouth. Those full, sensual lips I adore.

CONDUCTOR   Why did you have to be out there tonight, fatal beauty, or why did you have to be up there, faithful, adoring wife?

CONDUCTOR'S WIFE   Thank God for London. I couldn't bear another week without Ralph. I wonder what my husband would do if he knew about us. Kill me? Punish me through the children? Both. He's not a cruel man but a violent one. Listen to how he conducts *Le Sacre du Printemps*.

CONDUCTOR   Why couldn't tonight be next week in London? She won't be in London. She'll be with her lover.

YOUNG MAN   If not tonight, there's London. Surprised? She's not going to London. I'll be in the same seat at Festival Hall. I'll be at the Strand Palace, just across from the Savoy, where you've had the same river suite for years. I've done my homework. Bite! Your shirt's half open now.

CONDUCTOR   I'm doing the Mahler Ninth in London. I'm always so drained after the Mahler Ninth. Drained and horny. Someone . . . who was it? . . . someone said he'd fuck mud after the Mahler Ninth. James Levine but it sounds more like Lenny.

YOUNG MAN   They say if you stare at someone's left earlobe long enough, eventually they turn around. It burns a hole.

CONDUCTOR   It's all in the music. The longing, the yearning, the impossibility of . . . what? . . . love? No, it's something else. I am loved. I want to love but I've just never found anyone as interesting as me. As lovable. As worthy of my undivided attention. House left is one thing, her up there in her box is another. I'm talking about a whole other kettle of fish: the perfect fusion of two people. Two becoming one. Melting together, opening, succumbing, each subhuming the other. No, that's not the word. It's not even a word, *subhuming.* Each *sub*-what? the other! I know what I'm trying to say, I just can't find the word for it. When two people—!

CONCERTMASTER   He's lost again.

CONDUCTOR (*catching his mistake*)   Christ, that was close. (*He sees the Concertmaster glaring at him.*) He caught me. Stare him down. Give him the old "Don't even think of it, buster!" I know where I am. I always know where I am.

YOUNG MAN   Maybe it's the right earlobe.

CONDUCTOR   Who do you love the most? Who do you love the best?

CONCERTMASTER   You talking to me?

SURTITLE   *Höre ich nur diese Weise*
   Die so wundervoll und leise,

Wonne klagend, alles sagend,
Mild versöhnend aus ihm tönend
In mich dringet, auf sich schwinget,
Hold erhallend um mich klinget?
Heller schallend, mich umwallend,
Sind es Wellen sanfer Lüfte?
Sin des Wogen wonniger Düfte?

CONDUCTOR What is transfiguration but an orgasm coupled with a heart attack?

SURTITLE *Wie sie schwellen, mich umrauschen,*
Soll ich atmen, soll ich lauschen?
Sol ich schlürfen, untertauchen?
Süss in Düften, mich verhauchen?

CONDUCTOR This is not enough. Conducting it is not enough. Singing it is not enough. Writing it is not enough. Experience it. *Liebestod*, love-death. Love-death, *Liebestod*.

SURTITLE *In dem wogenden Schwall, in dem tönenden Schall,*
In des Welt-Atmens wehendem All
Ertrinken, versinken,
Unbewüsst, höchste Lust.

CONDUCTOR It's over already. I don't even remember it beginning.

Long pause as the music fades to absolute silence, the kind that follows a breathtaking, perfect performance.

CONCERTMASTER Well that's that. What's next? Oh, shit, the Bruckner Fourth.

CONDUCTOR'S WIFE Oh shit, the Bruckner Fourth. There is no God for a conductor's wife.

SOPRANO Isn't anybody going to clap?

YOUNG MAN   Now he's got to turn around. (*He stands and applauds.*) Bravo! Bravo!

This breaks the spell of the music and unleashes a tremendous ovation. Conductor doesn't move. Instead, he remains with his back to the concert hall audience.

Soprano accepts the ovation with appropriate humility.

Conductor suddenly turns to face the concert audience. Thus his back is to us now. He raises both arms for silence, which comes.

CONDUCTOR   Ladies and Gentlemen: I apologize for that decent but perfunctory performance of Wagner's sublime music. He deserves better, so do you. The fault was entirely mine. Not the orchestra's and certainly not our charming and accomplished soloist's. As Harry Truman said, "The buck stops here." So, to make amends, and with your kind permission, I propose a definitive *Prelude and Liebestod*. The *Prelude and Liebestod* Wagner imagined but to my knowledge has never been performed.

He turns back to the podium and the orchestra and raps his baton on the music stand in front of him.

CONDUCTOR   Again! From the top!

CONCERTMASTER   The whole thing again? And then the Bruckner Fourth? We'll be here till doomsday.

CONDUCTOR   Ladies and Gentlemen, you're either with me on this trip or you're not.

He raises both arms to give the downbeat.

CONDUCTOR'S WIFE   This is beyond the pale, even for him!

She will remain standing in her box, looking concerned, but will eventually sit.

YOUNG MAN   This is amazing. This is historic. This is him at his greatest. (*He sits.*)

SOPRANO   I did it the best I could the first time. I don't know what you want.

CONDUCTOR   You will, my dear, you will.

Soprano looks frightened but takes her seat. Conductor gives the downbeat and the opening chords of the Tristan Prelude flood the theater again. Very loud at first but eventually settling at the same volume as the previous rendition.

CONDUCTOR   Give them profile, lots of profile. They love your profile. Feed it to them.

YOUNG MAN   He saw me. Our eyes met.

CONDUCTOR   Move the body. They come for the body movement. Those fabulous, famous, far-reaching shoulders. Magnificent arms on a mighty torso. A photographer caught you with your shirt off after a Brahms Fourth and it was a picture seen around the world. High-flying adored. You and Evita! Move your ass for them. Tight firm buttocks worthy of someone half your age. Make them think about your cock and balls. Are they large? Is he clipped? Is he good? I'm terrific, baby. Ask her. Ask him. He'll give you an answer and he's only been there in his imagination.

CONDUCTOR'S WIFE   He keeps looking up. What is he trying to tell me?

YOUNG MAN   He is definitely looking.

CONDUCTOR   Ask anyone who's had the pleasure of my acquaintance. It's them who don't measure up. It's them who fail me. They're taking my strength, my passion but I'm getting nothing back. Where is my equal? My match?

I'm so alone up here. Everywhere I'm alone. I love this part. It's so deliberately ponderous. What is this music about? What is anything really about?

I don't think this is such a great passage right here but he's fucking Richard Wagner so I conduct it like I think it's a great passage. This is the last time I make you look good like this, you fucking anti-Semitic genius prick!

This music always makes me think of certain kinds of sex. Hot late-summer afternoon damp sheets sweaty grunting people outside blinds drawn dark dirty make it last as long as you can. Crazy, scream, rip the sheets, howl like a werewolf, hurt him, hurt her, ouchy kind of sex.

This will be in all the papers tomorrow. For twenty-four hours I'll be the most famous person in the world. Forty-eight maybe. Seventy-two. Then next week, when the magazines come out and the televisions have readied their investigations into *why*, there will be a new spurt of fame. Then a gradual subsiding. A plaque will go up somewhere. Probably outside this very hall. I won't be forgotten. She'll see to that. And God knows, no one anywhere ever again will listen to this music without thinking of me.

He looks at his wife. Their eyes meet and hold.

CONDUCTOR (*cont.*) You had the most beautiful skin and breasts and throat and everything when we met.

CONDUCTOR'S WIFE So did you, so did you.

CONDUCTOR They weren't enough.

CONDUCTOR'S WIFE Nothing has ever been enough for you.

CONDUCTOR You knew that when you married me.

CONDUCTOR'S WIFE I hoped the children would be enough.

CONDUCTOR We were wrong. They're not real.

CONDUCTOR'S WIFE Our children are real.

CONDUCTOR Not real enough. Real in themselves but not real to me. Not as real as this music. Nothing, no one is real enough. I am the only person in the world and I cannot bear the pain of being so alone.

CONDUCTOR'S WIFE Then I can't help you, my darling.

CONDUCTOR I'm only alive when I come—the way I want to be alive: ecstatic, half-conscious, eyes closed, brain flaring, words, thoughts inadequate.

CONDUCTOR'S WIFE Good-bye. We loved each other for a time. We were happy.

CONDUCTOR The only satisfying sexual experience I ever had was with a man.

His eyes have met the Young Man's; there is no mistaking it.

YOUNG MAN Finally. Talk to me, maestro.

CONDUCTOR At least I think it was a man.

YOUNG MAN Tell me all about it.

CONDUCTOR The kind of sexual experience this music is about.

CONCERTMASTER Now that's a tempo! This is more like it. I gotta hand it to him, when he's at his best, there's no one like him.

CONDUCTOR'S WIFE Go on, I'm listening.

CONDUCTOR I was twenty-two years old, studying in Florence. I'd already made my debut in Salzburg that summer, an instant sensation, the old fool broke his ankle playing *bocce* at his age! I took over, the Bruckner Fourth and the *Pathetique.* The Bruckner would have been next on the program. They're lucky they won't have to sit through it now. Nobody likes Bruckner. They just say they do. I loathe Bruckner, always have, even that afternoon in Salzburg when he put me on the map. Anybody could conduct the *Pathetique.* And they do, and they do. I was the toast of Europe. God, I was handsome that year. I could spend hours in front of the mirror talking to myself. I'd make faces. Scowl, smile. Flirt with myself. I could even get myself hard. This bastard . . . what was his name? . . . he was a journalist, political . . . the apartment was near the Piazza della Republica . . . it was over a pharmacy . . . *farmacia* . . . the steps were exhausting . . . deep, steep Renaissance steps . . . there was a terra-cotta Madonna in the apartment . . . he said it was a Luca Della Robbia and I wanted to believe him . . . I was already so famous but still so easily impressed. His very own Della Robbia! What the fuck was your name?

YOUNG MAN   Giorgio, Piero, Giacomo.

CONDUCTOR'S WIFE (*with a sigh*)   Ralph, Ralph, Ralph.

CONCERTMASTER   Asshole.

YOUNG MAN   Carlo, Mario, Fausto.

CONDUCTOR   Guglielmo! Guglielmo Tell. Be serious. Guglielmo Bianchini. He knew who I was. He must have. Everyone did. My picture was everywhere that summer. I was so beautiful that year—I was perfect—I was all I wanted—all anyone could ever possibly want—and this cocksucker, this arrogant wop, this goddamn glorious dago, he led me on and on and on. A touch, a glance, a brush of thigh, but no more. I wasn't even sure he was queer. Weeks went on like this. Torture. No one knew why I was staying on in Florence in the fearful heat. I'm doing research. What research? You know everything. It's true. I did. About music. But the promise of this person kept me there, prisoner.

CONDUCTOR'S WIFE   My poor darling.

YOUNG MAN   After the concert, when I ask for your autograph, I will pass you a slip of paper with my telephone number on it. No name, just a number. You'll know what to do with it.

CONDUCTOR   Finally, there was a weekend when his father, a widower and some sort of famous judge or lawyer, would be out of town at their place in Como. I went to the apartment. The door was ajar. There was no sign of him. I wandered through the empty apartment. It had been a palazzo. Everything was huge—molded, sculpted, ornate. I went into a bedroom—it must have been the father's—yes, that is where the Luca Della Robbia was, over an enormous bed, and I stood looking up at it, amazed, when I felt—I feel!—hands on me from behind. I didn't turn around. Don't want to.

The Soprano stands and begins to sing the Liebestod *again. This time the surtitles will be in English.*

CONDUCTOR (*cont.*)   Hands here, hands there. Hands over my eyes, hands over my mouth. Four hands. Someone else is there. I don't struggle. My clothes are being taken off— were being taken off—I don't know what tense I'm in— what tense I want to be in—the past is too remote, the present too frightening—and I am being stripped and stroked and I am blindfolded and I am led to the bed and

my cock is so hard and I am put on the bed and I let myself
be tied spread-eagle to it—no one has ever done this to me
and I do not resist—and when it is done I am left there for
what seems like hours and my hard-on will not subside and
once it even threatens to explode and I pray to the unseen
Della Robbia Madonna above me not to let me come and I
know this is blasphemy and I know that she forgives and
understands because she is a good mother—all mothers are
good mothers—and this is what mothers do and, oh, it is so
unimaginably intense to be there like that with him.

SOPRANO   How gently and quietly he smiles,
How fondly he opens his eyes!
See you, friends? Do you not see?
How he shines, ever higher,
Soaring on high, stars sparkling around him?
Do you not see?
How his heart proudly swells
And, brave and full, pulses in his breast?
How softly and gently from his lip
Sweet breath flutters:—
See, friends? Do you not feel and see it?
Do I alone hear this melody
Which, so wondrous and tender
In its blissful lament, all-revealing,
Gently pardoning, sounding from him,
Pierces me through, rises above,
Blessedly echoing and ringing round me?

CONDUCTOR   And after a while I am unblindfolded and see
my captors—Guglielmo and a young woman who can only
be his twin sister; she is a feminine mirror image of him—
and they are both nude and more beautiful than anyone I
have ever seen—more beautiful than even I was that

63

summer—and she straddles me and lowers herself onto my cock very slowly just once and I almost come but I pray and then he—Guglielmo—what an absurd name!—puts his mouth on my cock and moves it up and down the length of it just once and again I almost come and have to pray and then they both just looked at me and I said, "Please, make me come." "*Prego, fammi morire*" is what I said. "Please, make me die." I didn't know the Italian for come, you see, so I said, "*Prego, fammi morire,*" instead.

SOPRANO   Resounding yet more clearly, wafting about me,
Are they waves of refreshing breezes?
Are they clouds of heavenly fragrance?
As they swell and roar around me,
Shall I breathe them, shall I listen to them?

CONDUCTOR   And they just smile at each other. Guglielmo kisses one of her breasts. Francesca touches his cock. I'd named her by then, you see; I have a great need to know the names of things, especially people. Guglielmo and Francesca. I knew they weren't really twins. I wondered if they were even brother and sister. I didn't care. *Fammi morire.* She took her panties, pink, and ran them the length of my body, toe to head. Then she very slowly pushed them into my mouth, gagging me with them, letting me taste her. I didn't resist. The whole time our eyes held, mine and his, until he blindfolded me again. I felt their hands on me, their mouths. Everywhere. So close, but not yet, not yet! *Fammi morire!* I hear the door open and close. I don't care. I don't care about anything but this perfect moment which I want to last forever. Not yet, not yet. I stop thinking about the Madonna and praying to her and I can't hold back any longer and I come with an intensity that amazes me to this day and that I have never since, even remotely, equaled. I could feel my own semen on my lips, on my cheeks, in my hair.

CONCERTMASTER   This is beautiful. This is beautiful.

YOUNG MAN (*Rapturous*)   You're making me forget what I'm going to do to you. The music says it all.

CONDUCTOR'S WIFE   I love this man. I only deceive him sexually.

SOPRANO   Shall I sip them, plunge beneath them,
To expire in sweet perfume?

CONDUCTOR   Of course, after I came I lost all interest in the game and wanted to be free. More important, I lost all interest in them. I lay there feeling the flood of semen grow watery, then dry and caked on my stomach, chest, and face. Hours passed. I could not free myself. The blindfold, the gag held firm. Once, I relaxed enough to mentally relive the episode and I immediately got hard and came again, but not nearly so much this time. The next thing I knew I heard movement in the next room, the door opening and a woman's startled scream, then a man's angry voice and pretty soon I'm unblindfolded and the room is filled with people, most of whom are police, and an irate, bewildered couple in their sixties who had returned to their apartment after an outdoor performance of *Nabucco* in the Boboli Gardens and found me tied spread-eagle on their bed and who was I, how did I get there, what was I doing, or rather, what had I done? I never saw Guglielmo or Francesca again. It wasn't their apartment, of course. Were they even real? The orgasm was.

SOPRANO In the surging swell, in the ringing sound,
In the vast wave of the world's breath—
To drown, to sink
Unconscious—supreme bliss!

CONDUCTOR Once I asked my wife to tie me to the bed and sit on me. She loved it.

CONDUCTOR'S WIFE When he looks at me like that, who does he see?

CONDUCTOR Once I tied her. She loved it.

CONCERTMASTER I gotta hand it to you, asshole, we're cooking. This is the real thing.

CONDUCTOR Once I let a fan.

YOUNG MAN He can't keep his eyes off me.

CONDUCTOR Someone like you, sweetheart. But I'd had too much to drink or he'd had too much to drink or he smelled funny or he said something I didn't like—like in retrospect Reagan wasn't such a bad president—or he was too big or too little or one of the ten million other things that don't let you connect perfectly with another person. That hot August afternoon in Florence when I was young and beautiful and first famous and still thought the answer to a good and happy life was in my work, in other people, in success, seems so long ago. There is no other person to fill the void I have felt since then. There is a woman in a box who is my wife and bore me two children.

CONDUCTOR'S WIFE I love you. When all is said and done, I love you.

CONDUCTOR There is a young man, house left, who entertains fantasies about someone who he thinks is me.

YOUNG MAN   I know how you like it.

CONDUCTOR   There is a concertmaster who detests me.

CONCERTMASTER   You're still an asshole.

CONDUCTOR   But not half as much as I detest myself. There is a cow guest soprano who sings music that has no meaning for her in a perfectly ravishing voice.

SOPRANO   What did I do now?

CONDUCTOR   And so it goes. There are a lot of people. Five billion of us, I read just this morning, and pretty soon there will be six billion and the only time I ever felt connected to any of them was when I was twenty-two years old and tied spread-eagle to a retired Florentine optometrist's bed wanting to be made love to by two people I'm not even sure exist.

The last measures of the Liebestod *are sounding. Conductor holds his baton straight up in front of him with both hands. Then he turns it toward him and plunges it swiftly and deeply into his abdomen. Blood spurts onto the music stand. Conductor's face is transfigured.*

Another standing ovation has begun. Soprano bows deeply to the audience in the concert hall.

Young Man is already on his feet

Wife rises in her box, afraid. Soprano is relishing her ovation, oblivious. Conductor continues to stare straight ahead, blood spurting from him onto the music stand, a transfigured, ecstatic expression still on his face. The ovation is mounting.

BLACKOUT
THE END

Terrence McNally won Tony Awards for best play for *Love! Valour! Compassion!* and *Master Class,* as well as Tony Awards for best book of a musical for *Ragtime* and *Kiss of the Spiderwoman.* In addition, *Love! Valour! Compassion!* won the Drama Desk, Outer Critics Circle Award, and the New York Drama Critics' Circle Awards for best play. He also wrote the books for the musicals *The Full Monty, A Man of No Importance,* and *The Visit.* His other plays include *Corpus Christi,* which was named one of the best plays of 1998 by *Time* magazine; *A Perfect Ganesh,* a finalist for the Pulitzer Prize; *Lips Together, Teeth Apart; The Lisbon Traviata; Frankie and Johnny in the Clair de Lune;* and *It's Only A Play.* Earlier stage works include *Bad Habits, The Ritz, Where Has Tommy Flowers Gone?, And Things That Go Bump in the Night,* and the book for the musical *The Rink.* He has written a number of television scripts, including *Andre's Mother,* for which he won an Emmy Award. Mr. McNally has received two Guggenheim Fellowships, a Rockefeller grant, a Lucille Lortel Award, and a citation from the American Academy of Arts and Letters. A member of the Dramatists Guild since 1970, Mr. McNally was raised in Corpus Christi, Texas, and makes his home in New York City.